How to grow Banana Plants like a Professional

Beginner's guide and tips to get you started

Table of Contents

Introduction v

Banana Tree Growing Profile 1

    Botany...1

    Habitat 1

    Significance to Humans.......................................2

    Benefits of a banana plant 2

    What Banana plants like 3

    Banana plants dislike. 3

    Banana Species. 4

    Size and Shape. 4

    Exposure 5

    Foliage/Flowers/Fruit...5

    Additional Facts 5

    Design Tips...6

Land Preparation 7

    Field selection 8

    Cross-Pollination 8

    Sun and Good Soil 8

    Soil quality 9

Soil salinity or acidity 9

Surroundings...11

Space wisely...11

Growing tips..12

How do Bananas Grow? **15**

How to get Started with Growing Bananas.....................16

Planting Bananas 17

Maintaining your banana patch......................18

Growing banana fruiting........................ **21**

Pests & Diseases 23

Storage.. **25**

Conclusion.. **27**

Introduction

The Banana is one of the most produced and commercialized fruits in the world. According to the FAO (Food and Agriculture Organization of the United Nations), the area harvested in 2012 was approximately fine million hectares, and production was roughly 102 million tons. Brazil, India and the Philippines are the principal countries regarding the cultivated area, representing 722, 481 and 454 thousand hectares respectively. In 2011, international commercialization of banana embodied approximately 19 million tons of product. The main exporting countries were Ecuador, the Philippines, Costa Rica, and Colombia, while the main importers of the fruit were the United States, Belgium and eastern Europe.

Thus, the crop is essential to millions of families, most notably in various countries in Latin America and the Caribbean, where exportation of the product represents a significant source of income. In Brazil, the fruit is cultivated in all regions of the country, from north to south and covers an area of approximately 480 thousand hectares.

Several production methods characterize the banana culture, including the simplest manner of cultivation in which farmers merely collect the fruit, to highly sophisticated production systems designed to produce the banana for the external market using intensive labor, advance technology, and a vast number of chemical fertilizers.

To respond to the increasing demand and the expectations imposed by a competitive market, farmers are compelled to use substantial amounts of chemical fertilizers, pesticides, and other technologies which can cause severe negative impact upon both the environment and the health of millions of people, including farmers, workers, and consumers.

Taking all this into consideration, there is a growing interest from consumers, especially in northern countries, for responsible production and more equitable ways of marketing and distributing the product.

Considering this potential negative impact, while believing that it is possible to establish commercial relationships that promote social and environmental advancement , the Swedish Society for Nature Conservation(SSNC) requested a study comparing the two banana production systems - the organic and the conventional. For this book, then, an organic system s that which refrains from using chemical fertilizers or pesticides, while the conventional systems analyzed here are those that employ highly intensive chemical inputs and that is oriented toward servicing external markets. The main thrust of this book, then, it to compare these two systems – the organic and the conventional.

Banana Tree Growing Profile

Botany

Contrary to popular belief, banana plants are not trees but giant herbs, which reach their full height of between 10 and 20 feet after only a year. Every banana blossom develops into a fruit, which is ripe enough for consumption after about three or four months. After production fruit, the plants' stems die off and are replaced by new growth.

The number of bananas produced by each plant varies. However, ten or more bananas growing together forms a "hand." Banana stems have on average 150 "fingers" and weigh nearly 100 pounds. The trunks of banana plants are not woody, but composed of sheets of overlapping leaves wrapped tightly around one another, a design feature that enables them to conserve water.

Because banana plants are approximately 93 percent water, even moderate winds can knock them down and destroy entire plantations. Even a light wind can cause them to dry out and bake in the direct sunlight.

Habitat

Bananas are indigenous to the tropical portions of India, Southeast Asia, and northern Australia, and were brought to South

America by the Portuguese in the early 16th century. Today, banana plants grow in the humid, tropical regions of Central and South America, Africa, and Southeast Asia where there are high temperatures and rainfall. Modern agricultural technologies also enable people to cultivate banana plants in non-tropical regions such as California and Florida in the United States.

Significance to Humans

Grown in a very humid, the tropical region on Earth, bananas are the fourth most abundant fruit crop in the entire world and the most popular fruit in the United States. In Central and South America, bananas are vital to the economy. Most bananas sold in the United States originate from domestic farms. Banana leaves are used worldwide as cooking materials, plate, umbrellas, seat pads for benches, fishing lines.

Growing bananas does not take much effort, but it does require that you get a few things right when you first get started.

Benefits of a banana plant

- They make great windbreaks or screens
- They can keep the sun off the hot western or southern side of your house
- They utilize the water and nutrients in waste drains (think washing water or outdoor showers)
- The leaves can be fed to horses, cows and other grazers.
- The dried remains of the trunks can be used for weaving baskets and mats.

What Banana plants like

- Rich, dark, fertile soils.

- Lots of mulch and organic matter. LOTS. Just keep piling it on.

- Lots of nitrogen and potassium. (think chicken manure!)

- Steady warmth, not too hot and not too cold. (Bananas are sissies when it comes to temperatures...)

- Steady moisture, in the ground and in the air.

- The shelter of other bananas. That's the most overlooked aspect by home growers. Bananas grow better in the company of other banana plants.

Banana plants dislike.

- Strong winds.

- Extreme eat or cold.

- Being hungry or thirsty

- Being alone and exposed.

Banana trees are one of the common trees that come to mind when dreaming of the tropics. However, did you know that it it's not a tree? It is the world's most abundant herb. Still, due to its size, it is commonly thought of like a banana tree.

No matter what size your yard, there is a banana tree to fit it. While most species grow best in the warmer climates, there are cold-hardy banana trees.

The make excellent houseplants with enough light and water. While the fruit of many species is full of seeds and possibly inedible, cultivars have been created over time that eliminated the large seeds and made the fruit palatable.

Latin Name

The banana is a Musa spp. And it is part of the Musaceae family.

Common Names

It is commonly known as the banana or plantain.

Banana Species.

There are several varieties, but these are the most popular and most commonly grown.

- Cavendish is the variety that you know from the supermarkets. It's a stout variety that produces large massive brunches.

- Lady Fingers are very tall and slender plants and have sweeter fruit.

- Plantains are cooking bananas. They are drier and starchier. You use them green like you would use potatoes, and they taste similar. (80% of all bananas grown in the world are plantain varieties! They are an essential staple food in many tropical countries)

Size and Shape.

The plant size varies based on the cultivar chosen. "Truly Tiny' is only 1-1.5 inches call, while 'Cuban Red' can be up to 25-inches tall. Banana trees have an irregular shape.

Exposure

Grow in full sun for best results. In hotter areas, afternoon shade is welcome.

Foliage/Flowers/Fruit

Banana tree leaves are huge – depending on the species, they can be up to 2-inches wide and 9-inches long.

These trees are monoecious. There also may be neuter flowers. White flowers emerge from a purple bud.

Bananas are classified as a berry. The fruit comes from the female flowers, which, strangely enough. Develop without pollination. The fruit grows in a cluster, called a hand. Not all hands are edible for human consumption.

Other may be tastes but have large seeds. Sizes range from 2.5 – 12 inches long. The color can be yellow, pink, green or red.

Additional Facts

- The Eating banana commonly seen in stores is the 'Cavendish' variety.

- Bananas form in late summer. They don't start finally ripening until the following March. When they are green but plumped up, cut off the stalk and place in a cool, dry space.

- As stated before, bananas aren't trees since they have no wooden parts. The trunk is composed of the main fruiting stem enrobed by leaves.

Design Tips

Banana trees instantly bring a tropical eel to your garden. Grow in a location where it will be sheltered from the wind as they are very susceptible to damaged leaves. Use the banana trees a focal points of a background screen for your garden.

Land Preparation

When establishing a new banana grove, certain actions need to be implemented to ensure the long-term success of the grove. One of these steps involves the initial land preparation which should be done before transplanting of the plant material.

The purpose of land preparation is to provide the necessary soil conditions which will enhance the successful establishment of the young offshoots or the tissue culture plants received from the nursery.

The aim is to enable the grower to plan and structure the implementation process in advance, ensuring the successful establishment of the banana grove. Planning forms part of the initial preparation and will help to limit unnecessary stoppage or delays during the implementation phase.

Critical factors to consider during this planning exercise are summarized as follows:

- Availability and quality of irrigation water
- Field selection
- Mechanical action to be implemented
- Chemical needs for pre-plant soil improvement

- Tools and equipment required for banana cultivation

- Labor needs

- Irrigation design and installation

- Leaching schedule

- Financial requirements

- Schedule

- Rainfall runoff patterns

- morning and evening shade locations

Field selection

The area selected for the establishment of the new banana grove can influence the cost of the land preparation to the extent that it may not be viable to proceed with the development at all. The authors aim is to highlight the critical areas to be considered when selecting the land to grow your banana trees.

Cross-Pollination

Is a pollinator variety present? Cross-pollination by a different variety, of the same type of tree, is key to the success of many fruit trees. In most cases, its absence is why trees don't bear fruit or produce poorly.

Sun and Good Soil

Your banana plant would love a sunny place with well-drained, fertile soil that is protected from the wind. I do not recommend planting in heavy, pure clay soils.

Even if your yard isn't an ideal location, take heart. Banana plants are very adaptable and respond well to fertilizers, so the can get along even where the soil is nutritionally deficient. Just steer clear of sites with extremely heavy soils or very poor drainage.

Soil quality

Bananas grow in many parts of the world and can handle severe weather conditions, and can also be produced in different types of soil in both hot arid and semi-arid regions. You might be under the impression that the blazing temperatures of summer would be the end of banana tree, but it is actual temperatures at, or below freezing the will hurt or kill you banana plants. Fear not though, there are ways to ensure that your newly acquired banana plants grow, flourish and give you fruit for years to come.

The soil quality is related to its drainage capacity mainly when soils are salty, or a high salt content characterizes the irrigation water.

When evaluating the soil quality, give attention to:

- The soil texture which will influence the water retention capacity.
- The nutrient content to determine the corrective measures necessary for soil improvement.

Soil salinity or acidity

Plant growth is influenced by either saline or acid soil conditions which, in the end, will result in a loss of potential yield.

Saline and alkaline soils are common in banana groves and are characterized by a high concentration of soluble salts, and exchangeable sodium, respectively. Soluble salts present in these soils are sodium, calcium, magnesium, chloride and sulphate anions. Many high end garden shops will test your soil for trace amounts of these salts.

Saline soils have an electric conductivity (EC) of their saturated extract higher than 4 mmhos/cm at 25°C with a sodium absorption rate less the 15 and a pH less than 8.5. Saline soils can be recognized by the presence of a white layer on the surface of the soil resulting from the high salt concentrations which may harm the growth and development of your plant.

Alkaline soils are characterized by an EC of the saturated extract of less then 4 mmhos/cm at 25°C with a sodium absorption rate higher than 15 and a pH higher than 8.5. Alkaline soils do contain harmful quantities of alkalis within the hydroxyl group – OH, especially NaOH. These types of soil are usually difficult to correct coupled with a low production resulting from low content of calcium and nitrogen. However, it is recommended to eliminate the excess of sodium by the addition of acidifying agents (gypsum, Sulphate of iron, or Sulfur).

Saline and alkaline soils are usually the results of :

- An increase of the underground level of sodium caused by excessive drought conditions (high evaporation);
- The use of high salt content water
- Very poor drainage system.

When banana plants grow in climates of little rain, but high heat and much evaporation, irrigation or flood water evaporates quickly, and its salts are left on the surface of the soil. The negative influences of saline conditions are:

- High concentration of soluble salts

- High soil pH

- Poor drainage and aeration

- The adverse effects of sodium on the plant metabolism.

Surroundings

If you'd like your banana plants to become a landscaping asset, choose the planting place with this in mind. The crop yield may not be processional grade, but the esthetics will be very pleasing to the eyes. Imagine it as a full-grown plants and plot out everything. Wires overhead? Sidewalk or walkway near by? Does it obstruct something you want to see? Can you keep an eye on it from the house? Will other trees be in the way, allowing for their additional growth in the meantime?

Space wisely

First-time fruit tree growers often ask about recommend planting distances from patios, sewer lines, water pipers and so on. Ordinarily, patios will not be a problem because the soil beneath them will be dry and compacted. Therefore, the roots will not grow into this area as much. It is still recommended, however, that you plant at least 8-10 feet away from patios, and underground plants.

You can call the water company to come out and mark the locations of the water pipes and sewer lines, which most municipality do as a free service. You might not expect sewer and water lines to be affected since they are buried so deeply. But, since sewer and water lines tend to be wet, roots will grow to them and around them if the fruit tree is planted too close. By planting your trees far enough away from these items, you can avoid this problem.

The spacing between trees is as follows.

- Dwarf, 8-10 inches

- Semi-dwarf, 12-15 inches

- Standard, 18-25 inches

- Large 5-6 feet

- Giant 10-15 feet

Growing tips

Banana plants grow best in a fertile, well-drained soil. Salt is not tolerated. Banana plants prefer acidic soil. These trees need lots of water. However, you have to make sure they are not over-watered, so you don't get root rot. The soil should be moist but not soggy at all times if possible. Soil with excellent drainage will allow you to keep this moisture balance.

Banana plants should also be fertilized very well. Use a balanced fertilizer once a month n normal soil. Use a more specialized fertilizer if your soil is too acidic or too base. Consult a local garden store in your area. Spread the fertilizer evenly around the plant in a circle extending 4 to 8 feet from the trunk.

Do not allow the fertilizer to come in contact with the trunk. Wait till a banana plant is at least 3 feet tall and have developed their root system before your second fertilizing. Make sure there are several roots before you take any suckers off, so it doesn't unbalance the original plant.

How do Bananas Grow?

Bananas are perennial herbs. (Gingers, heliconias and bird-of-paradise flowers are distant relatives of bananas. They are all in the same order, Zingiberales.)

Banana trunks consist of all the leaf stalks wrapped around each other. New leaves start growing inside, below the ground. They push up through the middle and emerge from the center of the crown. So, does the flower, which finally turns into a bunch of bananas.

A banana plant takes about nine months to become fully grown and start producing a bunch of bananas. Then the mother plant dies. But around the base of it are many suckers, baby plants.

At the base of a banana plant, under the ground, is a large rhizome, called the corm. The corm has growing points, and they turn into new suckers. These suckers can be taken off and transplanted, and one or two can be left in position to replace the mother plant.

Great, so now you know what to do once you have bananas growing in your garden, but how do you start?

How to get Started with Growing Bananas

First you need to make sure that you can grow bananas where you are. You need a tropical or warm subtropical climate. Bananas can handle the extreme heat (if they have enough water), but they don't like it. They can handle cool weather for a short while, but they don't like that either. Below 14°C (57°F) they just stop growing.

If the temperature drops any lower the fruit suffers (the skin turns greyish) and the leaves can turn yellow. Frost kills the plant above ground, but the corm can survive and may re-shoot when the temperature rises again.

The ideal temperature range for banana growing is around 26-30°C (78-86°F). You need a lot of water to grow bananas. The enormous soft leaves evaporate a lot, and you have to keep up the supply. Bananas also need high humidity to be happy.

You need vibrant soil. If you don't have good soil to start with, make some. Incorporate lots and lots of compost and plenty of chicken manure before you plant your bananas (wood ash for extra potassium doesn't hurt either), and then mulch them very thickly. And just keep mulching and feeding the plants.

And you need room so you can plant enough of them together. Bananas need shelter from the wind. Growing many banana plants together increases the humidity in the middle, evens out the temperature changes a bit, and it shades and cools the trunks. You don't want to cook the flower that forming in the middle.

If you get a change to, look at a commercial banana planta-tion somewhere. The outside rows, especially the western side, always look sad. The best bananas grow in the middle rows.

You should plant bananas in blocks or clumps, not single rows and probably not individual plants. If you have very little room, you can grow a few banana plants together and grow something else on the outside to protect them. But you do need to give them that sheltered jungle environment if you want them to be happy.

Planting Bananas

You can not grow bananas from seed. Most banana plants don't produce seeds. The best way to start is with the suckers as mentioned earlier. Know someone who grows bananas? Talk to them, Every banana plant produces a lot more suckers than you need, so people usually have plenty to give away.

Only take suckers from vigorous banana plants. The suckers should have small, spear-shaped leaves and ideally be about four feet high. (Smaller suckers will take longer to fruit, and the fruit bunch will be smaller.)

Cut the sucker from the main banana plant with a sharp shovel. Cut downwards between the mature plant and the suck-er. You have to cut through the corm. It is not easy so make sure the shovel is sharp enough to cut and really put your strength into it.

Make sure you get a good chunk of corm and many roots with it. Chop off the top of the sucker to reduce evaporation while you move it and while it settles into its new home. (Remember, the growing point is at the bottom of a banana plant. You can decapitate the sucker. It will grow back.)

You can also dig up a bit of the corm and chop it into bits. Every bit that has an eye can be planted and will grow into a banana plant. But it takes longer that growing banana suckers.

Plant your bits or suckers in your well-prepared banana patch, keeping two to five meters between them.

The spacing depends on your layout. My banana plants grow in a block of several double rows. Within the double rows, the spacing is two to three meters, but there are two plants in each position, suckers of the first plant. And you have four to five meters between the double rows.

You can also have a banana circle around and outdoor shower where you only have two meters between individual plants, and they are growing haphazardly. And if you just want a single clump of a few banana plants you can put them even closer together.

Keep your banana plants moist but not too wet in the early days, or they may rot. (The don't have leaves yet to evaporate water, so they don't need much.)

Maintaining your banana patch.

The most common cause of death for bananas is lack of water. The most common cause of not getting fruit is starvation. Banana plants blow over in strong winds. Protect them and feed them and water them and all will be well. Other than that, bananas don't need much maintenance. Just remove any dead leaves and cut down the dead plants regularly.

You can get a better crop of bananas if you remove all the unwanted suckers, only keeping the best ones (select two for every vigorous healthy plant). The best suckers are the ones with the small, spear-shaped leaves. Remove the pretty ones with the big round leaves! Why? A sucer that is still fed by the mother plant does not need to have much photosynthesis, so it doesn't need to produce big leaves. And a sucker that is well looked after by the mother plant will produce better fruit and be stronger than one that has to struggle on its own.

A mature plantation is pretty much self-mulching. Just shred all the old leaves and trunks and throw the mixture back under the plants. You can also grow other plants in the understory to produce more mulch. (I use cassava, sweet potato, and herbs.)

You will need to sprinkle on some fertilizer now and then, to replace what the banana crop took out when harvested. Keep the fertilizer close to the trunk as bananas don't have a large root system.

Growing banana fruiting

You may see your first flower emerge after about six months, depending on the weather. Leave the leaves around it, especially the one protecting the top bend of the stalk from sunburn. A the purple flower petals curl back and drop off, they reveal a "hand" of bananas under each. Each banana is call a "finger".

You may get anything between four to a dozen or more full hands. Then, next petal, you'll see a hand of teeny weeny excuses for bananas. Those are the male fingers. The male fingers just dry and drop off. Only the stalk remains. If you let it grow, it will eventually reach the ground.

Some people break off the "bell" (the bunch of purple flower petals at the end) about 15 cm below the last female hand. That way the banana plant puts its energy and reserves into growing big bananas, and not into growing a long stalk. Commercial banana growers also remove some of the bottom female hands, so the remaining bananas grow larger.

When you have waited patiently for at least another two months. You may have to prop your banana bunch because it can become cumbersome, and a bunch can snap off or pull the whole plant over.

A good prop would be a long stick with a u-shaped hook at the end. But a long enough plank or pole can do the job, too. I'll leave that to your ingenuity.

Bananas are ready to be picked when they look well rounded with ribs, and the little flowers at the end are dry and rub off easily. They will eventually ripen on the bunch, and those bananas taste the best. But once they start to ripen, it happens very quickly, faster than you can eat or use them. So you may as well cut the top hands off a bit earlier and ripen them on the kitchen counter.

You can also cut the whole bunch and hang it somewhere if you need to protect it from possums or birds. But then all the bananas on the bunch will ripen at once, so be prepared.

You can preserve bananas for use in cooking and baking by peeling and freezing them. Or to preserve them for eating, peel , split in half lengthwise and dry them.

Once the bunch is picked the rest of the plant will die quickly. Cut it to the ground, throw some poo, and let the next suckers grow while you process all the bananas.

Tip: Commercial banana growers us bunch covers (plastic bags open at both ends that they slip over the bunch and tie at the top.) to protect bananas from diseases, insects, sunburn, and marauders. You can get the bogs at a rural supplies store, a local grower, or modify dry cleaning bags for the use.

Maintenance/Pruning

Before the banana tree fruits, prune so there is only one main stem. After it has been growing for 6 to 8 months, leave one sucker. This will replace the main stem in the next growing season. After the fruit is removed, cut the main stem down to 2.5'. Remove the rest of the stem in a few weeks, leaving the replacement sucker intact.

Pests & Diseases

Bananas are prompt for viral diseases, fungal diseases and pest thereby reduce production, quality, and yield. Otherwise, there are not many diseases or pests that affect the banana tree when grown outside of the tropics.

Pest	Viral Diseases	Fungal Diseases
Aphids (Pentalonia nigronervosa)	Banana Bunchy Top Virus	Head rot (Erwinia carotovora)
Fruit scarring battle (Besilepta subcostatum)	Banana Bract Mosaic Virus	Panama wilt (Furarium oxysporium)
Nematodes	Banana Mosaic Virus	Sigatoka leaf spot (Mycospharella spp)
Pseudostem weevil (Odaiporous longicolis)	Banana Streak Virus	-
Rhizome weevil (Cosmopolites Sordidus	-	-
Thrips (Chaetanaphotrips & signipennis & Heliaothrips kodaliphilus)	-	-

Storage

Keep Bananas refrigerated. The ripening process can be delayed if you refrigerate it. The skin of the fruit will turn dark, but the flesh remains firm. Conversely, do no store Bananas below 13°C as it will stop its ripening process all together (at that temperature Bananas o not emit heat or ethylene.)

Conclusion

On the other hand, if you consider yourself an avid gardener who enys the careful care of unusual plants from season to season banana plants make for a natural addition to the garden. If you already garden with other types of plants that grow from rhizomes, adding care of banana plants is not much a stretch.

If you like big, beautiful, lush tropical plants with vast, impressive greenery, a banana plant makes an excellent choice, indeed. You'll find some hardy banana plants to choose from, to amass a beautiful collection of various specimens if you desire.

In the final analysis, the best way to decide if you are going to grow banana plants is to try them. These days, these exotic beauties are affordable and easy to come by. With so many choices in care methods, a little trial and error will undoubtedly result in happy and successful banana plant-keeping!

Printed by Amazon Italia Logistica S.r.l.
Torrazza Piemonte (TO), Italy

10477844R00021